THE LITTLE
INSTRUCTION BOOK

Don't wear face packs in bed

OK let's start with the three R's:- Romance, relationships, rumpy pumpy.

First of all, chuck out all books that tell you about caring, sharing, hugging and communicating.

It's the small details of everyday living that make or break a relationship. Get them right, the soppy stuff automatically follows.

Let me clarify:
In your worst nightmare would you actually want:
- to hug someone who wears mustard Y fronts?
- communicate with someone who eats with their mouth open revealing half chewed broccoli to the whole restaurant?
- care and share with some arse who nicks the duvet every night?

I thought not. So get real. Read on for how to get the details right. And throw out the sick making advice books.

Appreciate the differences in the sexes,
don't try and change them so:

Don't mock when she says she's been to see a clairvoyant

Be patient when he won't stop and ask for directions

Always squeeze the toothpaste from the bottom
and put the top back on

At moments of passion,
don't tidy your discarded clothes into a neat pile

Remember men are not all the same
(though most are)

Don't get cross when he can't find his glasses
even when they're right in front of him

Don't interrupt, yawn or look around when she's speaking

Don't talk with your mouth full

Clean your teeth while they're still in your mouth

Don't make her sleep in the wet spot

Don't steal the duvet

Don't offer her the plug end of the bath

15

Warning!

Remember Durex have a sell by date

17

Sex appeal
HERS

- A bit of silk or lace can be more erotic
than nothing at all

- Take more interest in your lingerie
collection than your housework

Sex appeal
HIS

- Never wear nylon boxer shorts

- Stay well away from polyester safari suits

- Talking can be erotic,
but not about your prostrate operation

Don't confuse your birth control pills
with your hayfever tablets

Don't talk about ex lovers

Don't look for a meaningful one night stand

Don't give scores for performance

Don't wear stacks in shoes

Never wear a toupee

Wearing rubber doesn't mean the washing up gloves

Practising safe sex doesn't mean
when her husbands away OR
behind locked doors

Unless your partner is Mystic Meg
tell them what turns you on

Good in bed isn't lying still, not snoring

A woman's most receptive erogenous zone is her brain

Don't listen to the cricket commentary in bed

'Doing your thing'
does not mean making a great shepherd's pie

Don't worry about how often other couples do it
(or in what position)

29

Women are affected most by what they hear
Men are affected most by what they see

Of everything you wear,
your expression is the most important

Turn off's
HERS

Candlewick dressing gowns
Face packs in bed
Curlers in bed

Turn off's
HIS

Baggy Y fronts
Smelly socks
Vague replies

Celebrate Achievements

35

Don't ever blame each other
(blame your parents, teachers, the dog instead)

If you have to criticise,
don't wait for 'that right moment'
fax it through from a safe distance

Give her your last rolo

Drink enough to lose your inhibitions
but not so much you fall asleep
and can't remember a thing

Notice when she's made an effort
to lose some weight

Pretend not to notice when she's gained some

Don't eat toast in bed

Never sleep on an unfinished argument
Throw the bastard out for the night
And let him sleep elsewhere

Mark the calendar for when her period is due
then leave town for a few days

Take your socks off first when undressing.
There's nothing more ridiculous than the sight
of a naked man wearing only his socks.

Clear the air when it needs it
(this doesn't mean buy an air freshener)

Words your partner likes to hear:
I love you
I want you
Here's my credit card, spend what you like

Surprise your partner

Don't argue when she says
she has nothing to wear
even though her wardrobe's crammed to overflowing

Smile sweetly when she says
'Oh this old thing, I've had it ages,'
even though you know she bought it yesterday

Never cut off all your hair after an argument

Don't economise on luxuries:
Always buy:
good champagne, decent coffee
the best linen sheets
enormous luxurious bath towels

Don't leave it too long between treats

Never wear cheap perfume

Don't be horrible about each other's friends

Bathroom tips
HIS

Don't leave shaving stubble in the sink
after shaving

The loo does have a down position

Clean the bath after use

Bathroom tips
HERS

Don't use his razor to shave your legs

Don't leave knickers soaking in the sink
or stockings on the shower rail

Don't apologise for your body,
be proud of it

Love can satisfy all of the five senses:
sight, sound, taste, touch and smell:

SIGHT

Buy a Wonderbra

Never wear olive green or mustard underpants

Don't tuck your shirt in your underpants

Never have fluorescent lighting in the bedroom

SOUND

Listen to Sketches of Spain by Miles Davies

Indulge her taste in music

Give her a set of headphones for your Walkman

Do a tape of his favourite tracks

TASTE

Buy only the best icecream

Learn about fine wines

Raspberries are for eating not blowing

SMELL

Spray the sheets with your favourite fragrance

Fill the bedroom with scented candles

Don't eat so much that
whenever she has garlic mushrooms, she'll always thinks of you

TOUCH

Have a wonderful silk dressing gown

Silk, satin, velvet feel sensual,
crimplene doesn't.

Always compliment her appearance
before she goes out
(without being prompted)

Always let her know when
you're going to be late

Give each other a head or foot massage
with perfumed oil

Don't have killer toe nails

Don't take your digital watch into the bedroom

There are times to turn off your mobile

Always open your beer can away from her face

Always replace the empty toilet roll

Garlic/curry/onions are for both or neither

Close your mouth when you eat

If you have to give your willie a pet name,
keep quiet about it

Make a special breakfast

Think before having your nose pierced

Think twice before having your navel pierced

Think about an anaesthetic before
having anything else pierced

Think twice before having your nose pierced

Floss your teeth in private

Never pick your nose in front of each other

Don't look in her handbag

Don't leave the scrambled egg pan for her to do

Preserve the mystery

Take a large bowl of fruit to bed
(but nothing too spikey - like starfruit or pineapples)

Make sex fun

87

Don't bother pulling your tummy in
just before you get into bed,
she's going to see it anyway

Tempt the sexual palate,
steak may be nice on Monday,
but would you want it seven days a week?

It's not the length of the wand but the magic in the stick

Look into his eyes
(even if you're thinking of someone else)

91

Top on a woman's list of what she looks for in a man is
a sense of humour

Top on a man's list of what he looks for in a woman is
good looks, someone visually pleasing

When he's got a cold or flu,
he reverts to being a five year old,
who wants to be mothered and indulged.
Stay with a girlfriend til he's recovered

If you must shout at moments of excitement,
make sure you get the name right

Don't let the ironing pile up

Wait until hair disasters have grown back
before you say
'what the hell have you done to your hair?'

Always wear expensive smelling aftershave
Splash out on favourite bubble baths

Get a king size duvet

Girls don't always become their mothers

Laugh together
but choose your moment
(ie: not when he takes his trousers off)

Laugh at his best jokes,
again and again and again

Pick him up from the airport or station

Warm his side of the bed

Don't leave your make up all over the bedroom

Wait til you've known him a while
before you mention commitment

Wait til you've known him a long while
before you mention babies

Timing is essential
especially in a new relationship so:

Wait til you've known him a while
before you bring out the rubber thongs
and naughty nurse outfit

Have clean fingernails

Wear clean socks

Don't wear the shirt you wore the day before

Don't shovel your food

Don't do SBD's (silent but deadly's)
under the duvet

Impress your partner with a surprise
means organising champagne breaks
not wearing your arrow through the head hat

Don't complain when he sings his heart out in the bath
(even if all the notes are all out of tune)

Likewise when she spends hours in the bathroom

Don't wear saggy, baggy, underpants

Throw out grey unshapely lingerie

Never gasp in horror at her cellulite

Label video tapes

Do your share of housework
without having to be asked

Don't read his newspaper before
he's finished with it

Don't leave any of his records near the radiator

Put CD's back in their boxes

Pick up your clothes

Don't wear your walkman during sex

117

ALWAYS notice when she's been to the hairdresser

Never wear those enormous Garfield slippers
unless your love affair is over
and you can't find the words
to say goodbye

**MCNAUGHTY
BOOKS**

	£
The McNaughty Book of Limericks by Farquhar McNaughty	4.99
The McIrish Book of Logic by Seamus O'Really	4.99
The McVeggie Book of Rude Food by Squirty O'Gourd	4.99
The McTory Book of Bonks by Norman ffamily-Values	4.99
Victorian Cock-Ups and Other Stories by The Very Rev'd Steve Lovering	4.99
How to be a Politically Correct Sex Maniac by Johnny Condom	4.99
The Little Sexpot's Instruction Book	3.99

McNaughty Books are available from all good Book and Gift shops, or direct from the publishers John Napir Ltd. at P.O. Box 3353, London N1.